Fitness Ball Drills

The Body Coach Series

Fitness Ball Drills

Get Fit on the Ball with

Australia's Body Coach®

Paul Collins

Meyer & Meyer Sports

British Library Cataloguing in Publication Data
A catalogue record for this book is available from the British Library

Paul Collins
Fitness Ball Drills
Oxford: Meyer & Meyer Sport (UK) Ltd., 2007
ISBN 978-1-84126-221-5

© 2007 by Meyer & Meyer Sport (UK) Ltd.
Aachen, Adelaide, Auckland, Budapest, Graz, Indianapolis, Johannesburg, New York,
Olten (CH), Oxford, Singapore, Toronto
Member of the World
Sport Publishers' Association (WSPA)
www.w-s-p-a.org

Printed and bound by: B.O.S.S Druck und Medien GmbH, Germany
ISBN 978-1-84126-221-5
E-Mail: verlag@m-m-sports.com
www.m-m-sports.com

Introduction

Welcome!

Throughout our lives we learn a series of fundamental motor skills using balls of different sizes and shapes to help improve our balance, co-ordination, rhythm and timing. One ball in particular, the Fitness Ball (or Swiss Ball) – a large, round, lightweight exercise ball with anti-burst qualities – has been designed specifically for the demands of exercising.

Today, it is one of the most utilised pieces of gym and fitness equipment used throughout the world to tone, stretch and strengthen the whole body. The Fitness Ball is widely used by individuals involved in exercise, sports, personal training and rehabilitation as well as Pilates, Yoga and group exercise classes.

The Body Coach: Fitness Ball Drills provides a total body workout to help tone, strengthen and reshape your abdomen, arms, back, chest, buttocks and legs using a Fitness Ball. Unlike conventional exercise programs, *Fitness Ball Drills* allows you to gain strength and improve posture, balance, co-ordination and stability all at the same time. When exercising on a Fitness Ball your muscles contract in a manner that promotes body awareness and core-strength gains. You can workout just about anywhere on the ball: at home, on the job or at the gym.

Throughout this book you will find a series of exercises that target specific muscle groups. It is recommended that all exercises be learnt and supervised whilst under the guidance of a qualified fitness professional or physiotherapist and after gaining your doctor's approval and recommendations.

At the end of the book I have compiled a number of Fitness Ball exercise sample training routines that combine exercises together. More importantly, you now have an exercise reference guide on the ball showing the basic fundamentals that will help strengthen your whole body. I look forward to working with you!

Paul Collins
The Body Coach®

THE BODY COACH

Contents

About the Author

Paul Collins is an Award-winning Personal Trainer in Australia, a prolific author on fitness and weight loss topics and General Manager of the 'Australian Academy of Sport and Fitness', an International College in Sydney, Australia, specifically for overseas students wishing to study and obtain Fitness and Personal Training qualifications. His trademark coaching has been pioneered from a remarkable recovery from a chronic lower back injury, without drugs or surgery – inspiring thousands of people through appearances on TV, Radio and print media.

Coaching since age 14, Paul has personally trained world-class athletes and teams in a variety of sports, e.g., athletics, rugby, soccer, squash, tennis and many others including members of the Australian Olympic and Paralympic Swimming Teams. He is also a key presenter to the Australian Track and Field Coaching Association, Australian Swimming Coaches and Teachers Association, NSW Squash Academy and the Australian Fitness Industry.

Paul is an outstanding athlete in his own right, having played grade level in the national rugby league competition. He is also a former Australian Budokan Karate Champion, A-grade Squash player and NSW Masters Athletics Track & Field State Champion. As a leader in the field of personal fitness and weight loss, Paul has successfully combined a sports fitness background with Bachelor of Physical Education degree and international certification as a Strength and Conditioning Coach and Personal Trainer. As designer of *The Body Coach* book series, exercise products and educational programs, Paul travels internationally to present a highly entertaining series of Corporate Health & Wellbeing Seminars and exclusive Five-star Personal Training for VIPs.

To learn more visit: www.thebodycoach.com

Chapter 1

Fitness Ball Introduction

Stationary it looks like any other ball, just bigger. Endeavour to sit on it for the first time and you can expect a neuromuscular rodeo ride of hypothermic proportions.

Since movement efficiency is often determined by the ability to control muscular actions, anyone new to using a ball will expect a lot of movement with the aim of trying to maintain good balance.

Enter, the Fitness Ball. A large, lightweight, air-filled portable ball used as: an aid in general fitness, in prevention of back pain, and development in high level athletic training. Since the 1960s it has been used as a method in orthopaedic and Neuro-development treatment. Contributed as a safe and effective way of encouraging functional movement, increasing flexibility and in reducing episodes of back pain.

Movement effectiveness is often determined by our ability to control muscular contraction in all areas of our body in any given situation at any given time. In exercising on the Ball, you'll find yourself rewiring your nervous system – awakening hundreds of small stabilising muscles of the ankle, pelvis, torso, shoulder and wrist.

Balance and Co-ordination

Without any conscious effort, your body's muscular system is continually contracting and relaxing in order to sustain a sitting, front support, kneeling or standing position. Proprioceptors within the muscles and joints provide input necessary to make immediate adjustments in balance. The ability over time to accurately adjust to any changes in an unstable position indicates proficient balance and co-ordination – a characteristic elite athlete's tend to possess.

Physiotherapists recommend it for back pain patients as an alternative to a normal work chair – at the office. Providing a comfortable base of support, the body undergoes hundreds of small corrections, encouraging reflex responses that correct and improve posture. So, whilst sensory receptors stimulate muscles to improve body awareness you can add some fun to your day!

Highly versatile and adaptable to all age groups, ability levels and athletic and sporting situations you can easily design strength, flexibility and stability training programs. The greatest advantage of working out on the ball is that you find yourself exercising several muscle groups at once, especially the deep abdominal musculature. Which, in effect, is the closest you'll come to gymnastic training without doing any back flips.

Unquestionably, a well-developed core is the first step toward resolving structural imbalances and enhancing power transfer through efficient movement. Unlike traditional abdominal training, the Fitness Ball takes you through planes of movement that allow full range of movement in a variety of positions. Due to the unstable nature of the ball, you are compelled to be intrinsically aware of the positioning of your body. This unstable nature increases what athletes call the bodies 'kinaesthetic sense' – knowing where we are in space and time.

Athletes who may be strong in regular training programs can find Fitness Ball training challenging, especially if the majority of strength training is performed on machines. Puzzled! Even surprised! It soon becomes apparent the strength element that's been lacking in ones training program. Fixed axis weight machine training provides a good basis for muscle growth and lean muscle mass, but unfortunately limits the activation and recruitment of stabiliser and neutraliser muscle function, essential in protecting joints from injury.

Stabilisers are muscles that surround and protect joints from injury. Neutralisers are muscles that counteract the actions of other muscles to ensure smooth co-ordinated movements. So, when an athlete, used to fixed machine training is placed on a Fitness Ball, all the stabilisers and neutralisers are effectively brought into action and made to work. As a result, working in a totally unstable environment on the ball leads to high levels of nervous system activation.

Spinal Stability

The abdominal and lower back muscles play a dominant role in controlling posture, low back stabilisation, and total body balance. While large, multi-segmental muscles contribute the bulk of the stiffness to the spine, it is the small intersegmental muscles braced along the vertebrae that are primarily responsible for maintaining the stability of the spine.

Increasing the activity of the small muscles is seen to increase overall spinal stability. This highlights the importance of the motor control system to co-ordinate the muscle recruitment between the large and small muscles when handling small loads. This also points to the importance of improving

stabilisation mechanisms of the spine so that we can maximise the ability of the spine to protect itself from injury.

In simple terms, athletes need to know what muscles to use, when and where to use them and how much force to exert. Surprisingly not a lot of athletes have developed this ability to sufficient standard. This is a concern as core stabilisation (the ability to fix the torso in a static position) is a pre-requisite for safe and effective force application.

Due to the unstable nature of the Fitness Ball, you are compelled to be intrinsically aware of the positioning of the body. Continuous postural corrections and weight shifts assist in maintaining a stable position on the ball. This concept should initially be taught in a stable environment, by first simply sitting on the ball, before adding any motor co-ordination skills involving the arms and legs.

Postural Control

The engine room for force application is postural control. Correct posture during movement is seen to maximise resultant forces, whilst minimising the risk of injury. Understanding how to position ones body posture correctly – *controlling muscle function and alignment of the pelvis, torso, neck and head* – is central to all daily activities. Whilst all muscles of the torso are important in postural control, it's the deep back and abdominal musculature that seem to be the key. This is because of the role they play in fixing and aligning the vertebral column and pelvis.

Postural control through use of the Fitness Ball allows for greater summation of forces through efficient sequencing of muscles, fundamental in all sporting movements – baseball, cricket, golf, running, squash, swimming and tennis alike. Constant forces generated through the body via internal processes of muscular contraction increase balance, awareness and agility.

Selecting Exercises

Participants can sit, lie, lean, kneel and get into many other positions on a Fitness Ball, to perform exercises. Always begin with simple movements and build up to complex patterns involving finer motor control. Working on the ball demands your utmost attention, as any loss of concentration may ultimately result in a quick buck and throw.

Use the form principle – each exercise repetition and set should be performed perfectly until loss of form. Whether 2 or 20 repetitions, once the muscles and nervous system are fatigued, the quality will fall and the exercise is no longer beneficial. Remember, quality not quantity. A certified fitness professional or physiotherapist will be able to guide you with the number of repetitions and sets for each exercise or group of exercise.

Contraindications

Due to the instability of a Fitness Ball and the constant use of muscle groups to maintain balance, this may lead to quicker than expected fatigue, there are some people who may need to avoid various exercises, including:

- Persons who are fearful of falling
- Persons who do not feel comfortable on the ball
- Persons during the acute phase of a back pain episode
- Specific unstable spine injuries
- Spinal disease that can be exacerbated by the movements
- Cases where pain increases when using the ball
- Persons with any previous or current joint or muscular injury
- During pregnancy
- Periods of sickness, weakness, fatigue, pain or dizziness

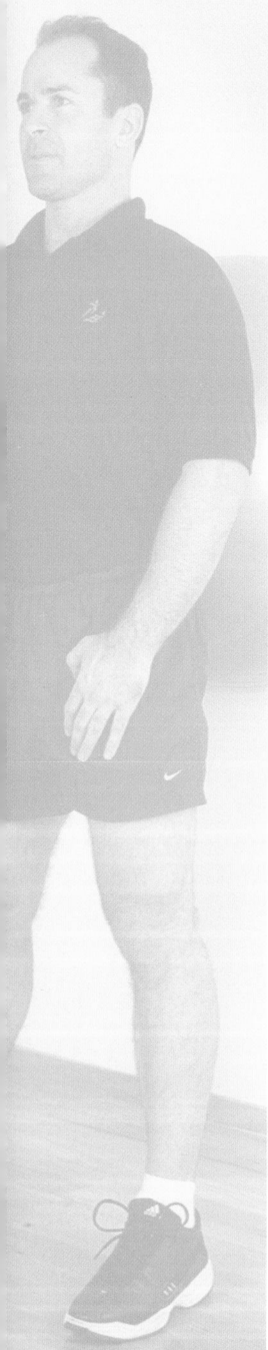

Precautions

As always, an important precaution is to seek the assistance of an appropriately certified fitness or health professional before starting and during any exercise program to ensure that you learn proper technique. It is also very important to gain approval and recommendations from your doctor. Ask your doctor about conditions that can be aggravated by this form of exercise before proceeding. Like any piece of equipment, follow all the manufacturer's instructions for care and use. Always do exercises in a controlled manner and speed; start slowly and build confidence.

Recovery

Due to a high neurological demand, neurological fatigue can be present despite no signs of metabolic fatigue. In other words, it is possible to reach muscle failure without showing any of the usual signs of physiological failure. When starting keep exercises to a minimum with up to 3 minutes rest between exercise sets. Care must also be taken not to advance in exercise selection too quickly. Therefore, keep it simple until mastery of body posture with each exercise before progressing in repetitions or sets.

Selecting a Ball

The Fitness Ball is available from a number of manufacturers in various sporting outlets fully inflated until it is firm at 55cm, 65cm or 75cm (20, 25 or 30 inches) sizes. As a general rule, when sitting on the 'Ball' the aim is for the legs to be parallel (legs at 90 degrees) or slightly above parallel with the ground. The following chart provides a good example when purchasing a ball:

Ball size		Body height	
55cm	20 inches	150-165cm	4.9-5.4 feet
25cm	25 inches	165-185cm	5.4-6.1 feet
75cm	30 inches	185cm +	6.1 + feet

Note: *In any situation, always adhere to the manufacturers recommendations and guidelines.*

Getting Started

Find a flat, open, non-slip area clear of debris. When first sitting on the ball, it is most important that you feel balanced and comfortable. Allow your buttocks to sink into the centre of the ball. Use your hands for balance on the side of the ball and place your feet shoulder width apart for good support – this will build confidence (further described in Chapter 2 – Sitting on the Ball). Understanding the function of the muscles involved is important from a standpoint of total body awareness. Initially, you will have to make a conscious effort to apply this control through pelvic control, spine, head and neck positioning, abdominal bracing and deep breathing. As you become proficient, correct body positioning will become automatic.

Working with a certified fitness professional, coach or physical therapist is recommended as part of Fitness Ball Basics. Their role is to help demonstrate the exercise, support your movement patterns and re-align the body to ensure correct movement patterns are performed. This approach will help maximise exercise gains in terms of balance, co-ordination, strength and muscle synergy. See Chapter 10 for establishing reps, sets and rest and fitness ball routines.

Let's get the ball rolling!

Chapter 2

Sitting on the Ball

Learning to sit properly on a fitness ball provides the positional awareness for other exercises that follow. As basic as it may seem, the goal is to sit directly in the centre of the ball in order to maintain ones centre of gravity. Before sitting on the ball ensure it is stationary, on a flat, non-slip surface with a clear area around you. Stand with your back to the ball, feet shoulder width apart and rear of legs touching the ball.

Keep one hand on the ball at all times to maintain proprioceptive awareness and positioning of the ball. When sitting, bend the knees and slowly lower sitting directly in the centre of the ball. This may require multiple foot, hip and body adjustments.

Once sitting on the fitness ball, lengthen the torso without leaning backwards or forwards, instead upright. Slow, small movements from side-to-side or circles from the hip in either direction whilst sitting on the ball will help bring confidence and awareness in using the ball. Focus on how the muscles are reacting to bring awareness to your mind and body. It is the finer details of each exercise including body position and movement that makes all the difference when exercising on the ball.

In the beginning and throughout your development, most exercises require you to work slow and under tension whilst maintaining good body posture. This ensures the correct muscle firing patterns are achieved. The objective is to master the basics before moving onto more advanced exercises. Progression can generally be determined by ones ability to maintain correct body posture throughout the exercise.

The challenge itself comes from being able to hold good posture performing a number of exercise repetitions and sets. So, what's easy for one person maybe hard for another. That's why it's recommended that all exercises on the fitness ball be demonstrated and taught under the guidance of a certified coach, fitness professional or physiotherapist.

These specialists will be able to determine how many repetitions and sets you should perform whilst also adjusting and correcting the body to ensure you maintain good form.

The following exercises aim to assist with developing good body posture, balance and co-ordination when sitting on the ball. This helps establish the confidence and motivation for performing other exercises and developing core-strength, body awareness and muscle tone.

Single Knee Lift

Description

- Find your position on the centre of the ball
- Place both hands on either side of the ball for support
- Sit tall and brace your abdominal muscles
- Keep your feet your-width apart
- Keeping your abdominal muscles braced, slowly lift one knee up and foot off the ground.
- Most importantly, maintain square hips at all times without leaning to the side, forwards or backwards
- Raise the knee and foot slowly until 30cm off the ground, hold, then slowly lower and repeat with the opposite leg.
- Keep the movements slow and controlled with deep breathing pattern
- Start and finish with the foot in the same position – avoid any lateral movement or positional change
- The coach stands behind the ball for support

THE BODY COACH

Description

- Utilise same sitting position as with Single Knee Lift exercise (above)
- To enhance the intensity of the exercise raise the arms to the side until parallel to the ground – for balance
- Slowly lift the knee and extend the leg forward until the leg is straight. Reverse movement and lower leg. Repeat with the opposite leg
- Avoid leaning forward, sideways or backward. Remain tall throughout, keeping the hips square and abdominal muscles tight
- Start and finish with the foot in the same position – avoid any lateral movement or positional change
- The coach stands behind the ball for support

Variation
- *With the leg extended and body position upright, the coach can challenge the athletes' balance and co-ordination by gently pushing the ball on either side. This makes the athlete have to adjust using their deep postural muscles*

3

Single Knee Lift with Leg and Arm Extension

Start

Midpoint

Description

- Sit tall on the ball with feet parallel and arms back by your side

- Simultaneously, lift one knee and extend the leg whilst extending your arms forward

- Maintain an upright body position. Avoid leaning forward, sideways or backward – remain tall throughout, keeping the hips square and abdominal muscles tight

- Return leg and arms back to starting point and repeat with opposite leg

- Start and finish with the foot in the same position – avoid any movement or change

- Start with slow controlled movements in order to maintain good body posture

- Maintain deep breathing pattern throughout

- The coach stands behind the ball for support

Note: *For optimal gain on the fitness ball, start with slow controlled movements to allow you to regularly adjust your body position to ensure correct posture and strength is developed. Overtime, through regular participation, one may gradually increase the speed of movement for a cardiovascular training effect.*

Coach Challenge

When sitting or lying on the ball, the coach can challenge the participant by gently moving the ball from side-to-side or back and forth with small movements. The participant is challenged whilst exercising on the ball by having to constantly re-adjust their body position.

Chapter 3

Abdominal Exercises

The following exercises are designed primary to strengthen the abdominal muscles, which help support the spine and development of good body posture. Commonly referred to as the 'core region' or 'power house', the abdominal muscles form a cylinder around the spine between the ribs and pelvis. In order to strengthen these muscles, exercises need to be performed slow and under tension with good pelvic control whilst breathing deeply. The challenge is placed on the abdominal muscles themselves in either a contracted (static) position or working them through a shortening and lengthening motion and at varying angles. The anterior muscles between the ribs and pelvis are known as the rectus abdominus whilst the side abdominal muscles are termed the abdominal obliques.

Focusing on the finer details of each exercise, your body position, movement and muscle control will help you gain optimal benefit. Learn to master the basics before progressing to a more advanced exercise or those requiring longer leverage. The body is also placed in a number of different positions on the ball that may require additional support from other muscles of the body including the chest, arms, shoulders, back and leg muscles. There should be no stress or tension on the lower back region. Ensure direct instruction, guidance and support from a qualified fitness professional or physiotherapist at all times to ensure correct movement patterns are learnt.

Abdominal Roll-ups

Start

Midpoint

THE BODY COACH

Emphasis

- Abdominal strength and endurance

Description

- Lie on back, knees bent, holding fitness ball on stomach
- Contract the abdominal region as you slowly roll the fitness ball up the legs to the knees, then lower
- Maintain constant contraction of the abdominal muscles until the exercise set is completed

Teaching Points

- Gently brace abdominal muscles and hold throughout whole exercise
- Maintain head in neutral position – avoid bringing chin to chest
- Raise and lower for count of 3
- Maintain deep breathing pattern throughout movement patterns
- Breathe out when rolling up
- Breathe in when lowering body down

FITNESS BALL DRILLS

Start

Midpoint

Emphasis

- Abdominal strength and endurance

Description

- Lie on ball, supported under lower back
- Feet shoulder-width apart, arms bent at 90 degrees by side
- Contract the abdominal region and slowly extend arms forward as you raise the body to form dish position between the hip and shoulder region
- Breathe in and slowly lower keeping the muscles activated
- Maintain constant contraction of the abdominal muscles until the exercise set is completed

Teaching Points

- Gently brace abdominal muscles and hold throughout whole exercise
- Maintain head in neutral position – avoid bringing chin to chest
- Raise and lower for count of 3
- Maintain contact of lower back on ball
- Maintain deep breathing pattern throughout movement patterns
- Breathe out when curling stomach and raising body
- Breathe in when lowering body down
- Avoid movement of the feet, leg angle, your bottom and the ball

Start

Midpoint

Emphasis

- Abdominal strength and endurance

Description

- Lie on ball, supported under lower back
- Feet shoulder-width apart, arms bent with hands behind head
- Contract the abdominal region and slowly raise the body to form dish position between the hip and shoulder region
- Breathe in and lower keeping the muscles activated
- Maintain constant contraction of the abdominal muscles until the exercise set is completed

Teaching Points

- Gently brace abdominal muscles and hold throughout whole exercise
- Maintain head in neutral position – avoid bringing chin to chest or elbows together
- Raise and lower for count of 3
- Maintain contact of lower back on ball
- Maintain deep breathing pattern throughout movement patterns
- Breathe out when crunching stomach and raising body into dish
- Breathe in when lowering body down
- Avoid movement of the feet, leg angle, your bottom and the ball

Start

Midpoint

Emphasis

- Abdominal strength and endurance

Description

- Lie on ball, supported under lower back
- Feet shoulder-width apart, arms extended above head, hands together.
- Contract the abdominal region and slowly raise the body to form dish position between the hip and shoulder region
- Breathe in and lower keeping the muscles activated
- Maintain constant contraction of the abdominal muscles until the exercise set is completed

Teaching Points

- Gently brace abdominal muscles and hold throughout whole exercise
- Maintain head in neutral position – avoid bringing chin to chest or arms forward of eye-line.
- Raise and lower for count of 3. Maintain contact of lower back on ball
- Maintain deep breathing pattern throughout movement patterns
- Breathe out when curling stomach and raising body into dish
- Breathe in when lowering body down
- Avoid movement of the feet, leg angle, your bottom and the ball

Oblique Twist

Start

Midpoint

THE BODY COACH

Emphasis

- Abdominal oblique strength and timing

Description

- Lie on ball at shoulder height with hips raised and body parallel to ground.
- Feet shoulder-width apart, arms extended above chest, hands together.
- Contract the abdominal region as you slowly twist the body, lower the arms to the left side – simultaneously bending at the knee and rotating the hip, torso and shoulders across the ball until arms parallel to ground.
- Keeping arms extended, rotate across the ball to the right side.

Teaching Points

- Gently brace abdominal muscles and hold throughout whole exercise
- Fitness ball to move underneath body as shoulders twist
- Twist onto shoulder on ball. Bend knees to accommodate movement
- Move head in time with body and in line with shoulder in neutral position. Twist slowly under tension for count of 3 to each side
- Maintain deep breathing pattern throughout movement patterns
- Add weight to hands (i.e. medicine ball) to increase intensity

Oblique Crunch

Start

Midpoint

THE BODY COACH

Emphasis

- Abdominal oblique strength and timing

Description

- Lie on ball, supported under lower back and feet shoulder-width apart
- One-arm bent with fingertips resting against head and the other arm extended above head – body slightly rotated
- Contract the abdominal region as you slowly raise the body, extending the arm up and across in midline with the opposite knee, then lower.
- Perform set and repeat on opposite side with opposite arms bent and extended

Teaching Points

- Gently brace abdominal muscles and hold throughout whole exercise
- Maintain contact of lower back on ball
- Raise and lower slowly for a count of 3
- Maintain deep breathing pattern throughout movement patterns
- Maintain head in neutral position keeping the muscles activated
- Breathe out when curling stomach and raising body
- Breathe in when lowering body down
- Avoid movement of the feet, leg angle, your bottom and the ball

Start

Midpoint

Emphasis

- Abdominal (upper, oblique and lower) strength and timing

Description

- Lie on ball, supported under lower back
- Feet shoulder-width apart, one-arm extended above head, the other arm holding the ball for support
- Contract the abdominal region as you simultaneously raise the extended arm and opposite leg to midline of the body, then lower.
- Perform set and repeat on opposite side

Teaching Points

- Gently brace abdominal muscles and hold throughout whole exercise
- Maintain contact of lower back on ball
- Ensure good foot placement and arm position holding the ball
- Raise and lower slowly for a count of 3
- Maintain deep breathing pattern throughout movement patterns
- Maintain head in neutral position
- Breathe out when curling stomach and raising leg
- Breathe in when lowering body down
- Avoid movement of the ball

Start

Midpoint

Emphasis

- Abdominal (oblique) and Quadratus Lumborum strength

Description

- Legs straddled in lunge position with outer leg back, rest on side of ball from hip to arm pit
- Arms bent, one resting on waist the other on side of head.
- Keeping the torso long, slowly contract muscles and bend side up from ball, then lower
- Perform set and repeat on opposite side

Teaching Points

- Gently brace abdominal muscles and hold
- Maintain contact of hip on ball and good foot stability
- Raise and lower slowly for a count of 2
- Maintain deep breathing pattern throughout movement patterns
- Breathe out when bending up
- Breathe in when lowering body down
- Avoid movement of the ball

Prone Roll-out – Short Lever

Start

Midpoint

THE BODY COACH

Emphasis

- Abdominal (core) and shoulder strength

Description

- Kneel on ground – thighs vertical, body angled at 45 degrees – fists clenched resting side-by-side on top of ball
- Keeping the body tight and elbows in close, slowly roll the ball forward until forearms resting across ball and body is long
- Hold briefly, and then return back to starting position

Teaching Points

- Gently brace abdominal muscles and hold throughout whole exercise
- Avoid arching lower back or slumping across shoulders
- Maintain strong arm and shoulder contraction
- Keep hands (fists) together and elbows close
- Extend and return slowly for a count of 3
- Maintain deep breathing pattern throughout movement patterns
- Breathe out when extending forward
- Breathe in when returning back

Variation

- Prone Roll-out – Long Lever (on toes)

13

Prone Isometric Holds

Start

Midpoint

Emphasis

- Abdominal (core) and shoulder strength

Description

- Kneel on ground – thighs vertical, body angled at 45 degrees – fists clenched resting side-by-side on top of ball.

- Keeping the body tight, slowly roll the ball forward, raising the pelvis and knees and positioning the upper body parallel to the ground

- Rest on forearms and toes, with feet shoulder-width apart.

- Hold for brief period (i.e. 3 – 20 seconds) then lower to starting position

Teaching Points

- Gently brace abdominal muscles and hold throughout whole exercise

- Avoid arching over lower back or through shoulders

- Maintain strong arm and shoulder contraction

- Keep hands (fists) together and elbows close

- Maintain deep breathing pattern throughout movement patterns

Variation

- As strength and core-stability improves, raise one leg a few inches off the ground to increase the exercise intensity, keeping the hips square and lower back in neutral position

Abdominal Exercise Summary

The majority of exercises performed on the Fitness Ball challenge the abdominal region. This exercise summary includes drills that isolate the abdominal muscles. By learning the basic fitness ball fundamentals within this book provides the foundation for more challenging drills that may arise in the future.

4. Abdominal Roll-ups

5. Abdominal Reach

6. Abdominal Crunch
   – Short Lever

7. Abdominal Crunch
   – Long Lever

THE BODY COACH

8. Oblique Twist

9. Oblique Crunch

10. Oblique Cross-over

11. Side Flexion

**12. Prone Roll-out
– Short Lever**

13. Prone Isometric Holds

Chapter 4

Lower Back, Hip and Leg Exercises

The following exercises combine strengthening the posterior or rear region of the body including the lower back, hip and legs. The body is placed in a number of different positions on the ball that may require additional support from other muscles of the body including the chest, arms, shoulders, back and abdominal muscles in performing these exercises. Each exercise should be performed in a slow controlled manner whilst breathing deeply and without any muscular tension or pain.

The challenge placed on these muscle groups is either static or working them through a range of motion. Focusing on the finer detail of each exercise, your body position, movement and muscle control will help you gain optimal benefit. Learn to master the basics before progressing to more advanced exercises requiring a longer lever or smaller base of support. Ensure direct instruction, guidance and support from a qualified fitness professional or physiotherapist at all times to ensure correct movement patterns.

14

Trunk Extension – Short Lever

Start

Midpoint

THE BODY COACH

Emphasis

- Strengthen lower back

Description

- Lie on ball on stomach, with knees shoulder-width apart, arms bent, fingers resting against side of head
- Keeping the body extended, raise the chest off the ball, and then lower

Teaching Points

- Gently brace abdominal muscles and hold throughout whole exercise
- Keep elbows wide
- Avoid arching lower back – keep torso long
- Raise and lower slowly for a count of 3
- Maintain deep breathing pattern throughout movement patterns
- Breathe out when raising
- Breathe in when lowering

Start

Midpoint

Emphasis

- Strengthen lower back

Description

- Lie on ball across hip, with hands on ground in front-support (push-up position) and toes resting on ground
- Ensure equal balance between all 4 ground touch points – hands and feet
- Bracing the abdominal muscles, slowly raise arms up off the ground until extended in line with body, and then lower

Teaching Points

- Gently brace abdominal muscles and hold throughout whole exercise
- The body will rebalance its centre of gravity as the arms rise. This will become the working range of motion
- Avoid arching lower back
- Raise and lower slowly for a count of 3
- Maintain deep breathing pattern throughout movement patterns
- Breathe out when raising
- Breathe in when lowering

Alternate Raises

Start

Midpoint

THE BODY COACH

Emphasis

- Strengthen lower back and co-ordination

Description

- Lie on ball across hip, with hands on ground in front-support (push-up position) and toes resting on ground
- Ensure equal balance between all 4 ground touch points – hands and feet
- Keeping the body tight, simultaneously raise one leg and opposite arm in-line with the body, then lower and repeat opposite arm and leg

Teaching Points

- Gently brace abdominal muscles and hold throughout whole exercise
- Avoid arching lower back
- Work at maintaining strong core and balance on ball
- Raise and lower slowly for a count of 3
- Maintain deep breathing pattern throughout movement patterns
- Breathe out when raising
- Breathe in when lowering

Start

Midpoint

Emphasis

- Strengthen lower back and hip region

Description

- Lie on back on ground with legs slightly bent and heels resting on ball
- Extend arms on ground at 45-degree angle to side of body for support
- Contracting the abdominal region, slowly raise the hips off the ground until in-line with body – straight line from shoulders to feet
- Hold briefly and then lower

Teaching Points

- Gently brace abdominal muscles and hold throughout whole exercise
- Avoid arching lower back or sinking
- Work at maintaining strong core and balance on ball with feet and on ground with arms
- Raise and lower slowly for a count of 3
- Maintain deep breathing pattern throughout movement patterns
- Breathe out when raising
- Breathe in when lowering

Note: *Start with shorter lever by resting calves on ball before increasing the challenge of the drill by resting your heels on the ball*

Start

Midpoint

Emphasis

- Strengthen lower back and hip region

Description

- Lie on back on ground with legs slightly bent and heels resting on ball
- Extend arms on ground at 45-degree angle to side of body for support
- Bend elbows and raise hands into air to shorten lever length and support – to increase the intensity of the exercise
- Contracting the abdominal region, slowly raise the hips off the ground until in-line with body – straight line from shoulders to feet
- Hold briefly and then lower

Teaching Points

- Gently brace abdominal muscles and hold throughout whole exercise
- Avoid arching lower back or sinking
- Work at maintaining strong core and balance on ball with feet and on ground with shortened arm levers
- Raise and lower slowly for a count of 3
- Maintain deep breathing pattern throughout movement patterns
- Breathe out when raising
- Breathe in when lowering

19 Leg Curls

Start

Midpoint

Emphasis

- Strengthen lower back, hip and hamstrings (leg) regions

Description

- Lie on back on ground with legs slightly bent and heels resting on ball
- Extend arms on ground at 45-degree angle to side of body for support
- Bend elbows and raise hands into air to shorten lever length and base of support – to increase the intensity of the exercise
- Contracting the abdominal region, slowly raise the hips off the ground until in-line with body
- Keeping the body tight, use the heels to slowly roll the ball towards the buttocks – flexing the legs until 90-degrees and then return to starting position
- **Note:** *Extend and flatten the arms back onto the ground for additional balance and support*

Teaching Points

- Gently brace abdominal muscles and hold throughout whole exercise
- Avoid arching lower back or sinking
- Work at maintaining strong core and balance on ball with feet and on ground with arms
- Keep heels firmly planted with pressure down into ball
- Flex and extend legs each for a count of 2
- Stop exercise if any lower back tension or pain arises
- Maintain deep breathing pattern throughout movement patterns
- Breathe out when flexing legs
- Breathe in when straightening

FITNESS BALL DRILLS

Start

Midpoint

Emphasis

- Strengthen lower back, hip and hamstrings (leg) regions

* Advanced exercisers only

Description

- Lie on back on ground with legs slightly bent and heels resting on ball
- Extend arms on ground at 45-degree angle to side of body for support
- Bend elbows and raise hands into air to shorten lever length and base of support – to increase the intensity of the exercise
- Contracting the abdominal region, slowly raise the hips off the ground until in-line with body
- Raise one leg off the ball ensuring hips remain square and abdominal muscles braced
- Keeping the body tight, flex the single leg on the ball towards buttocks until 90-degrees and then return to starting position
- Complete set, rest and repeat with opposite leg on ball
- **Note:** *Extend and flatten the arms back onto the ground for additional balance and support*

Teaching Points

- Gently brace abdominal muscles and hold throughout whole exercise
- Avoid arching lower back or sinking
- Work at maintaining strong core and balance on ball with one leg and on ground with arms. **Note:** *Lower hands to ground for added balance and support (leverage), if required.*
- Keep raised leg straight and hips square
- Keep heel firmly planted with pressure down into ball
- Flex and extend legs each for a count of 2
- Stop exercise if any lower back tension or pain arises
- Maintain deep breathing pattern throughout movement patterns
- Breathe out when flexing leg
- Breathe in when straightening

Start  **Midpoint**

Emphasis

- Strengthen leg and hip muscles

Description

- Stand with feet shoulder-width apart and ball behind back against wall
- Start with ball positioned in neutral position of lower back
- Place hands on front of thighs for support
- Simultaneously bend at hip, knee and ankle and lower to ground until legs at 90-degrees
- Return to upright starting position

Teaching Points

- Gently brace abdominal muscles and hold throughout whole exercise

- Lower and raise each for a count of 3

- Keep knees over midline of toes

- Avoid knees rolling inwards and heels raising off ground

- Stop exercise if any lower back or knee tension or pain arises

- Maintain deep breathing pattern throughout movement patterns

- Breathe out when rising

- Breathe in when lowering

Note: *As the legs become stronger, start with the feet closer to the wall and the ball positioned across the mid-back region. In the first instance, it may feel as though you are leaning forward, but this will ensure a more efficient squat pattern. The goal is to imitate a body weight squat pattern with shoulders, hip, knee and ankle aligned with the feet directly under the body.*

Start

Midpoint

Emphasis

- Strengthen leg and hip muscles

Description

- Stand with feet shoulder-width apart and ball behind back against wall
- Start with ball positioned in neutral position of lower back
- Raise arms parallel to ground and extend one leg forward
- Simultaneously bend at hip, knee and ankle and lower to ground until leg at 90-degrees
- Return to upright starting position
- Repeat set with opposite leg

* Advanced exercisers only

Teaching Points

- Gently brace abdominal muscles and hold throughout whole exercise

- Lower and raise each for a count of 3

- Use short-range movement only when first beginning. As strength improves gradually increase leg angle depth towards 90-degrees

- Keep knees over midline of toes

- Stop exercise if any lower back or knee tension or pain arises

- Maintain deep breathing pattern throughout movement patterns

- Breathe out when rising

- Breathe in when lowering

- Always have coach assist with this movement

Lower Back, Hip and Leg Exercise Summary Chart

14. Trunk Extension
    – Short Lever

15. Trunk Extension
    – Long Lever

16. Alternate Raises

17. Supine Hip Extension
    – Beginner

18. Supine Hip Extension
– Int/Adv

19. Leg Curls

20. Single Leg Curls

21. Squat

22. Single Leg Squat

Chapter 5

Chest
and Arms

The following exercises focus on strengthening muscles of the chest, arm and abdominal regions. The body is predominantly in a front support position, resting on the hands and feet. The abdominal muscles require ongoing activation in order to effectively support ones body weight as the lever length increases, helping reduce the load placed on the lower back region. If this element is lost at any time throughout the movement, body re-adjustments need to be made or the exercise is stopped due to bad form. Ensure the head and neck remain in alignment with the body at all times. To reduce wrist tension for participants first starting, the wrists maybe strapped or clenched fists used to keep wrist alignment straight.

Each exercise should be performed in a slow controlled manner whilst breathing deeply and without any muscular tension or pain. The challenge is placed on these muscle groups either statically or working through a range of motion. Focusing on the finer detail of each exercise, your body position, movement and muscle control will help you gain optimal benefit. Learn to master the basics before progressing to a more advanced exercises or movement patterns involving longer levers. Ensure direct instruction, guidance and support from a qualified fitness professional or physiotherapist at all times to ensure correct movement patterns are learnt.

Exercise 23-25:

Prone Walkout Series

23

Level 1: Beginner – Short Lever
with thigh support

Start

Midpoint - thigh

THE BODY COACH

Start

Midpoint - ankle

25

Level 3: Advanced – Long Lever
with toe support

Start

Midpoint – on toes

Emphasis

- Strengthen arm, chest, shoulder and abdominal muscles

THE BODY COACH

Description

- Lie on ball on hip, with hands on ground in front-support (push-up position) and toes resting on ground
- Keeping the body tight through strong abdominal brace, simultaneously walk hands forward whilst ball rolls across stomach and hip to:

  Level 1: Thigh or shin

  Level 2: Ankle

  Level 3: Up onto toes

- Hold for one full breathe at mid-point then return back to starting position ensuring a tight body position is held at all times.

Teaching Points

- Gently brace abdominal muscles and hold throughout whole exercise
- Avoid arching lower back when walking out and back on hands
- Ensure good head and neck alignment is maintained at all times
- Continually re-adjust stomach, head and neck alignment and hip position to ensure neutral spinal position is maintained
- Work at maintaining strong core and balance on ball by controlling the speed of movement at all times
- Maintain tension on legs and core area until exercise is finished
- Start by mastering Level 1: Beginner in both a static holding position and through range of movement, then gradually work towards maintaining good posture and body position in level 2 and 3.
- Maintain deep breathing pattern throughout movement patterns
- This exercise can be advanced by raising one leg off the ball as shown in the front support hold exercise that follows

Front Support Holds

26   Level 1: Front support hold

27   Level 2: Hold with one leg raised

Exercise 26 – Level 1: Beginner/Intermediate
Exercise 27 – Level 2: Advanced

THE BODY COACH

Emphasis

- Strengthen arm, chest, shoulder and abdominal muscles

Description

- Lie on ball on hip, with hands on ground in front-support (push-up position) and toes resting on ground
- Keeping the body tight through strong abdominal brace, simultaneously walk hands forward whilst ball rolls across stomach and hip to:

  Level 1: Shin or Ankle

  Level 2: Shin or ankle with one leg raised

- Hold body position for 1-5 deep breaths at mid-point (Level 1 or 2)
- Return back to starting position with stomach resting on ball, ensuring a tight body position is held at all times.

Teaching Points

- Gently brace abdominal muscles and hold throughout whole exercise
- Avoid arching lower back when walking out and back on hands and holding stationary position
- Continually re-adjust stomach, head and neck alignment and hip position to ensure neutral spinal position is maintained
- Work at maintaining strong core and balance on ball by controlling the abdominal region and leg tension
- Maintain tension on legs and core area until exercise is finished
- Start by mastering Level 1: Beginner, then gradually work towards maintaining good posture and body position in level 2.
- Maintain deep breathing pattern throughout movements

FITNESS BALL DRILLS

Start – Arms extended

Midpoint – lower chest to ball

Emphasis

* Strengthen chest and arm muscles whilst holding strong core

Description

- Lie on stomach on ball with legs extended on toes on ground and hands positioned on side on ball
- Brace abdominal muscles and ensure head is forward of hands
- Breathing out, push-up off the ball, extending the arms keeping the body tight until fully raised
- Breathe in and slowly lower chest down towards ball ensuring the spine is held in its neutral position
- Repeat push-up action

Teaching Points

- Gently brace abdominal muscles and hold throughout whole exercise
- Ensure a tight body position is held at all times
- Avoid any arching of lower back
- Continually re-adjust stomach, head and neck alignment and hip position to ensure neutral spinal position is maintained
- Maintain head in forward position of hands and in neutral position
- Work at maintaining strong core and balance on ball through hands arms, cheat and abdominal muscles
- Maintain deep breathing pattern throughout movement patterns
- Breathe out as you raise
- Breathe in as you lower

Variation

- If this exercise is too demanding, continuing strengthening the upper body with front support holds and prone walkouts.
- Alternatively, place the ball against a wall, kneel on the ground and perform kneeling push-up until you become stronger

Start

Midpoint

Emphasis

- Strengthen arm, chest, shoulder and abdominal muscles

Description

- Lie on ball on hip, with hands on ground in front-support (push-up position) and toes resting on ground
- Keeping the body tight through strong abdominal brace, simultaneously walk hands forward whilst ball rolls across stomach and hip to:

  Level 1: Shin or ankle

  Level 2: Up on toes (as shown)
- Hold extended body position and breathe deeply
- Ensure abdominal muscles are braced and good position is held, roll ball forwards towards chest by bending knees, then outwards to starting position

Teaching Points

- Gently brace abdominal muscles and hold throughout whole exercise
- Maintain weight forwards on hands, chest and arms as knees come under body
- Continually re-adjust stomach, head and neck alignment and hip position to ensure neutral spinal position is maintained
- Work at maintaining strong core and balance on ball by controlling the arm, abdominal and leg tension
- Maintain tension on legs and core area until exercise is finished
- Keep knees under body throughout movement pattern
- Start by mastering Level 1: on Shin or ankle, then gradually work towards maintaining good posture and body position in Level 2.
- Maintain deep breathing pattern throughout movement patterns
- Breathe out when extending legs
- Breathe in when bringing knees to chest

Advanced Prone Jack-knife* – Single Leg

Start

Midpoint

Emphasis

- Strengthen arm, chest, shoulder and abdominal muscles

* Advanced exercisers only

THE BODY COACH

Description

- Lie on ball on hip, with hands on ground in front-support (push-up position) and shin resting on ball
- Keeping the body tight through strong abdominal brace, simultaneously walk hands forward whilst ball rolls across stomach and hip onto shin and ankle region
- Raise one leg and hold ensuring hips remain square
- Roll ball forwards towards chest by bending knee of leg on ball
- Extend leg back to starting position
- Complete set and repeat with opposite leg

Teaching Points

- Gently brace abdominal muscles and hold throughout whole exercise
- Maintain weight on hands, chest and arms as knee comes under body
- Continually re-adjust stomach, head and neck alignment and hip position to ensure neutral spinal position is maintained
- Work at maintaining strong core and balance on ball by controlling the arm, abdominal and leg tension
- Maintain tension on legs and core area until exercise is finished
- Keep knees under body throughout movement pattern
- Maintain deep breathing pattern throughout movement patterns
- Breathe out when extending legs
- Breathe in when bringing knees to chest

Incline Push-ups

31

Level 1:   Beginner – Short Lever
with shin support

Start – On Shins

Lower chest to ground

THE BODY COACH

Level 2: Intermediate – Long Lever with ankle support

Start – on ankles and lower chest towards ground

Level 3: Advanced – Long Lever with toes support

Start Point – on toes and lower chest towards ground

Emphasis

- Strengthen arm, chest, shoulder and abdominal muscles

Description

- Lie on ball on hip, with hands on ground in front-support (push-up position) and toes resting on ground
- Keeping the body tight through strong abdominal brace, simultaneously walk hands forward whilst ball rolls across stomach and hip to:
  Level 1: Thigh or shin
  Level 2: Ankle
  Level 3: Up onto toes
- Maintaining a tight body position, lower your chest towards the ground by bending the arms to 90 degrees, before rising up to the upright starting position.

Teaching Points

- Gently brace abdominal muscles and hold throughout whole exercise
- Maintain weight on hands, chest and arms – keeping head forward of hands when lowering and raising
- Avoid arching lower back with body extended
- Work at maintaining strong core and balance on ball by controlling the speed of movement at all times
- Maintain tension on legs and core area until exercise is completed
- Start by mastering Level 1: Beginner, then gradually work towards maintaining good posture and body position in level 2 and 3
- Maintain deep breathing pattern throughout movements
- Breathe out as you raise and breathe in as you lower
- **Note:** *Master front support holds before attempting push-up variations.*

Variation

- In Level 1 Front Support Position, gently roll ball from side-to-side with feet and lower back tension to challenge the abdominal core region

THE BODY COACH

Start

Midpoint

Emphasis
- Strengthen chest, arms, shoulders and abdominal muscles

Description
- Lie on the ball and walk arms forward into front support position with hands shoulder-width apart and thighs and knees resting on ball
- Keeping the body tight, contract and raise the pelvis (buttocks) into the air as your legs roll along ball
- Raise up until torso is vertical with feet resting on ball
- Slowly lower in a controlled manner back to front support position

Teaching Points
- Gently brace abdominal muscles and hold
- Lift hips and maintain leg tension
- Avoid bending the arms or legs
- Maintain strong arm and shoulder contraction throughout
- Extend and return slowly for a count of 3
- Maintain deep breathing pattern throughout movement patterns
- Ensure support from a certified professional to perform this exercise

* Advanced exercisers only

Chest and Arms Exercise Summary Chart

Combination drills that link one exercise to another can be introduced once the basics foundation has been established. For instance, the prone walk-out exercise may include one or a series of push-ups at the mid-point position to increase the exercise challenge before walking hands and body back to lie on ball. Through regular participation you will find a number of exercises that can be linked together.

23. Prone Walk-out – Level 1

24. Prone Walk-out – Level 2

25. Prone Walk-out – Level 3

26. Front Support Holds – Level 1

27. Front Support Holds – L2

28. Push-ups

29. Prone Jack-knife

30. Advanced Prone Jack-knife

31. Incline Push-up – Beginner

32. Incline Push-up – Int.

33. Incline Push-up – Advanced

34. Prone Abdominal/Hip Raise

FITNESS BALL DRILLS

Chapter 6
Balances

All exercise on a fitness ball requires some form of balance to control the movement pattern. Previously you have utilized exercises that strengthen a particular muscle group using the hands and feet as a base of support. This section provides drills focused specifically on improving balance utilizing a number of body positions that challenge ones centre of gravity whilst balancing on the ball. The ability overtime to accurately adjust the body to any changes in unstable body position indicates proficient balance and co-ordination.

Performing balance exercises, the body undergoes hundreds of small corrections, encouraging reflex responses that help correct and improve posture. Hence, focus on the finer detail of each exercise, as well as your body position, movement and muscle control whilst continuing to breathe deeply. Learn to master the basics first before progressing to the intermediate level and more advanced exercises.

The following balance exercises are demonstrated on the ball without support for picture clarity only. Hence, read all instructions. All balances should be performed under the guidance and support of a certified fitness professional or physiotherapist – supporting the athlete and ball throughout the whole movement in order to stop participants from falling.

Balances may vary in length of time, being held from 5 to 90 seconds or more, or until loss of form. Maintaining good body position on the ball is the key to success.

Beginner

35 Seated Balance

Seated

Description

- Sit on ball and brace abdominal muscles
- Slowly raise legs off ground and use arms to assist balance
- Coach stands behind participant to support balance
- Maintain deep breathing pattern

THE BODY COACH

Extend one leg

Description

- Sit on centre of ball with arms extended and feet shoulder-width apart

- Brace abdominal muscles and raise arms to the side of the body and parallel to the ground

- Slowly raise one leg off the ground, keeping the hips square and body upright – avoiding any sideways or forwards and backwards movement

- Coach stands behind participant to support balance

- Maintain deep breathing pattern

Lying on Stomach

Description

- Lie on ball across stomach and hip region with hands and feet on ground
- Slowly raise arms and legs off ground and balance
- Coach stands behind participant to support balance
- Maintain deep breathing pattern

Intermediate

Prone Elbow Support

Prone Elbow Support

Description

- Place ball against wall for support
- Athlete stands behind ball
- The coach stands to the side of participant and ball for support
- Start with forearms across ball; hands together in the centre of ball whilst resting on knees
- Raise up onto toes and brace abdominal muscles and hold position whilst breathing deeply
- Maintain balance through strong abdominal brace, shoulder, arm and leg tension

Note: *To increase intensity raise one leg a few inches off the ground and hold, keeping the hips square at all times*

Supine Bridge

Supine Bridge

Description

- Lie on back on ball resting across shoulders and feet on ground with legs at 90-degree angle

- Keep hips square

- Brace abdominal muscles and raise one leg until parallel to ground and hold

- Lower leg and repeat opposite side – keeping the ball still

- Extend arms to side to assist with balance

- Coach stands to the side of athlete and ball for support

- Maintain balance through strong abdominal brace, shoulder, arm and leg tension

- Maintain deep breathing pattern

Advanced

Kneeling

Kneeling

Description

- Place ball against wall
- Athlete stands behind ball
- Coach stands behind ball and athlete for support
- Using the wall for support with hands, the athlete places one knee up on ball, then the other – knees apart, resting on ball across shin area
- Raise arms to the side to assist balance
- Maintain balance by keeping hips slightly bent, maintaining a strong abdominal brace and arm and leg tension

Note: *Picture demonstrates kneeling balance without wall support, as a progression once competent*

Level 2: Side Support (shown)

Description

- Place ball against wall for support
- Athlete stands on one side of ball
- Coach stands on the other side of ball to support athlete
- **Level 1:** Kneeling on ground beside the ball, the athlete rests forearm across centre of ball and hold
- **Level 2:** Extend from kneeling position onto side of feet with forearm across centre of ball and hold (as shown)
- The coach stands behind athlete and ball for support
- Maintain balance through strong abdominal brace, shoulder, arm and leg tension and straight body alignment
- Repeat balance on opposite arm
- Maintain deep breathing pattern

THE BODY COACH

Kneeling – one leg

Description

- Athlete stands behind ball
- Coach stands beside athlete
- Place both hands on either side of ball followed by one leg and then the other – across shins.
- Slowly raise one leg and extend keeping hips square
- Keep hips square – avoid raising leg too high, arching back or twisting hips
- Maintain balance through strong abdominal brace and arm and leg tension
- Repeat with opposite leg raised
- Maintain deep breathing pattern

Balance Exercise Summary Chart

Balances may vary in length of time, being held from 5 to 90 seconds or more, or until loss of form. Maintaining good body position on the ball is the key to success.

35. Seated Balance

36. Leg Extended

37. Lying on Stomach

38. Prone Elbow Support

THE BODY COACH

39. Supine Bridge

40. Kneeling

41. Side Support

42. Single Leg Balance

Chapter 7

Strength
Training

The Fitness Ball adds a new dimension to strength training by increasing the stability mechanisms required whilst performing each exercise. Not only is the target muscle area strengthened, so are the deep supporting muscles required to maintain the body's stability when exercising on the ball. For this reason, strength training exercises on the ball are limited to advanced level exercisers only, who have obtained a good strength base.

As each fitness ball is manufactured differently, only selected fitness balls with a manufacturers guarantee are suitable to perform weighted exercises on. Most quality ball manufacturers specify the actual load the ball can handle. In many instances the ball is also anti-burst resistant – for example: the ability to hold up 500 kilograms/1100 lbs. When using hand weights on a certified anti-burst ball however, never exceed your body weight as the load. If the ball you are using does not have a load rating, the quality is generally poor and exercising on this ball is not recommended.

The following exercises demonstrate those often used by athletes to strengthen the chest, back, shoulders, biceps and triceps muscles. The body is placed in a number of different positions on the ball that may require additional support from other muscles of the body including the abdominal, lower back, hip, gluteal and leg muscles. Each exercise should be performed in a slow controlled manner whilst breathing deeply and without any muscular tension or pain.

The challenge is placed on these muscle groups either statically or working through a range of motion. It is important to focus on the finer detail of each exercise – your body position, movement and muscle control – to help you gain optimal benefit.

Ensure direct instruction, guidance and support from a qualified fitness professional or physiotherapist at all times to ensure correct movement patterns are learnt.

Chest Flyes

Start

Midpoint

THE BODY COACH

Emphasis

- Strengthen chest muscles and core stability

Description

- Lie on ball, supported under mid to upper back region with feet shoulder-width apart and arms extended above eyeline
- The coach places light hand weights in your hands, and then kneels down to support movement from behind the ball
- Breathing in lower arms out to the side in arch motion to gain stretch across chest
- Breathe out and bring hands up and back together above eyeline

Teaching Points

- Gently brace abdominal muscles and hold throughout whole exercise
- Maintain your head in neutral position with your body
- Maintain constant contraction of the abdominal muscles until the exercise set is completed
- Raise and lower each for a count of 2
- Maintain good foot placement on ground and body position on ball
- Maintain deep breathing pattern throughout exercise – breathing in as you lower your arms and out as you raise them

Start

Midpoint

THE BODY COACH

Emphasis

- Strengthen mid back and shoulders

Description

- Place hand weights on ground in front of ball
- Lie on ball on stomach with legs extended and resting on toes
- Brace stomach and hold body position in straight line
- Reach down and grab hand weights keeping knuckles facing forwards and arms shoulder-width apart
- Bend elbows and lift arms to side until parallel to ground, then lower
- Maintain arm alignment with chest region

Teaching Points

- Gently brace abdominal muscles and hold throughout whole exercise
- Maintain your head in neutral position with your body
- Maintain constant contraction of the abdominal muscles and straight body position until the exercise set is completed
- Raise and lower each for a count of 2
- Maintain good foot placement on ground and body position on ball
- Maintain deep breathing pattern throughout exercise
- Breathe in whilst lowering the arms
- Breathe out whilst lifting the elbows

Start

Midpoint

Emphasis

- Strengthen biceps (arm) muscles

Description

- Kneel on ground and lie across ball on stomach
- Extend arms forward with triceps muscle and elbow resting on ball and palms facing upwards
- Brace stomach and hold body position
- The coach places light hand weights into hands and supports movement pattern from in front of the ball
- Bend arms and raise weights towards chin whilst breathing out
- Lower and extend arms whilst breathing in

Teaching Points

- Gently brace abdominal muscles and hold throughout whole exercise
- Maintain your head in neutral position with your body
- Raise and lower each for a count of 2
- Maintain deep breathing pattern throughout exercise
- Breathe in whilst extending arms
- Breathe out whilst bending elbows and bringing weight towards chin

Start

Midpoint

Emphasis

- Strengthen chest, arm and abdominal muscles

Description

- Lie on ball, supported under lower back region with feet shoulder-width apart and arms extended above eyeline
- The coach places light hand weight into hands, and then kneels down to support movement from behind the ball
- Grip weight with both hands and maintain slight bend in arms
- Breathing in lower weight overhead and down until parallel to ground
- Breathe out and raise weight up until back above eyeline

Teaching Points

- Gently brace abdominal muscles and hold throughout whole exercise
- Maintain your head in neutral position with your body
- Maintain constant contraction of the abdominal muscles until the exercise set is completed
- Avoid over arching the lower back region
- Raise and lower each for a count of 2
- Maintain good foot placement on ground and body position on ball
- Maintain deep breathing pattern throughout exercise

Start

Midpoint

Emphasis

- Strengthen shoulder and arm muscles

Description

- Sit on ball and maintain balance with feet shoulder-width apart and abdominal muscles braced
- Bend arms out to side with hands in line with chin
- The coach places light hand weights in your hands, and then supports movement from behind the ball
- Ensure abdominal muscles are braced to avoid lower back arching
- Breathing out extend arms up and above head bring hands together in a slight arcing motion
- Breathe in bend elbows and lower back to side

Teaching Points

- Gently brace abdominal muscles and hold throughout whole exercise
- Avoid arching of the lower back and movement on ball
- Maintain your head in neutral position with your body
- Maintain constant contraction of the abdominal muscles until the exercise set is completed
- Raise and lower each for a count of 2
- Maintain good foot placement on ground and body position on ball
- Maintain deep breathing pattern throughout exercise

FITNESS BALL DRILLS

Start

Midpoint

Emphasis

- Strengthen chest muscles and core stability

Description

- Lie on ball, supported under mid to upper back region with feet shoulder-width apart and arms extended above eyeline

- The coach places light hand weights in your hands, and then kneels down to support movement from behind the ball

- Ensure abdominal muscles are braced with arms extended and weight in hands

- Breathing in lower arms out to the side in arcing motion to gain stretch across chest – triceps muscles and elbows touching the ball

- Breathe out and push weight back up and together above eyeline in small arching motion

Teaching Points

- Gently brace abdominal muscles and hold throughout whole exercise

- Maintain your head in neutral position with your body

- Ensure arms and hands remain in line with chest throughout movement

- Maintain constant contraction of the abdominal muscles until the exercise set is completed

- Raise and lower each for a count of 2

- Maintain good foot placement on ground and body position on ball

- Maintain deep breathing pattern throughout exercise

Start

Midpoint

Emphasis

- Strengthen chest muscles and core stability

Description

- Lie on ball, supported under mid to upper back region with feet shoulder-width apart
- Extend both arms up above eyeline with one hand open and the other hand clenched and brace abdominal muscles
- The coach places light hand weight in open raised hand and then kneels down to support movement from behind the ball
- Lower unweighted hand and find centre of gravity on ball with body
- Breathing in lower weighted arm down by bending at the elbow and moving shoulders across the ball whilst simultaneously extending opposite arm high into the air for counterbalance
- Breathe out and push weighted arm back up above eyeline whilst simultaneously moving shoulders across the ball and bending opposite elbow into ball for added support and counterbalance

Teaching Points

- Gently brace abdominal muscles and hold throughout whole exercise
- Maintain your head in neutral position with your body
- Maintain constant contraction of the abdominal muscles until the exercise set is completed
- Raise and lower each for a count of 2
- Maintain good foot placement on ground and body position on ball as ball moves under shoulder region
- Maintain deep breathing pattern throughout exercise

FITNESS BALL DRILLS

Strength Training Exercise Summary Chart

43. Chest Flyes

44. Incline Rows

45. Biceps Curls

46. Pull-overs

THE BODY COACH

47. Shoulder Press

48. Chest Press

49. Single Arm Chest Press

Chapter 8

Functional Body Rotations

Functional body rotations combine many of the skills learnt on the ball at varying angles and move these into a rotational movement pattern. Exercises performed on the ball on the back, side and front on the body form the basis that builds the strength and motivation to master functional body rotations. In my experience, the ability to apply a functional body rotation drill in a straight line over 10–20m whilst controlling the speed is a good sign of exercise competence on the ball. But before you go out and try this, you must master the basics first under the guidance of a fitness professional or physiotherapist.

Athletes who grew up participating in sports involving rotation such as gymnasts will have an added advantage over others due their enhanced proprioceptive (body) awareness of rotation. Any rotational element adds a totally new dimension to an exercise or movement pattern and must be taught in small segments that break the exercise down. The outcome of mastering these smaller steps is a test of ones ability to control the body; it's muscle and the speed whilst on the ball.

It is important that a clear, flat open space such as a wooden sprung basketball court or football oval be used to perform these drills. Focusing on the finer detail of each exercise, your body position, movement and muscle control will help you gain optimal benefit. Learn to master the basic 180-degree rotational pattern before progressing to the more advanced 360-degree rotation and attempting the 10m test. Ensure direct instruction, guidance and support from a qualified fitness professional or physiotherapist at all times to ensure correct movement patterns are learnt.

Functional Body Rotations – 180°

1. Start

2. Midpoint

3. 180° Rotation

Emphasis

- Muscular balance, co-ordination and timing in rotation

Description

- Lie on ball, supported under lower back
- Feet shoulder-width apart, arms extended out to the side, parallel to ground
- Simultaneously turn chest and arms together to the left side whilst taking left leg under the right leg in rotation
- As the body rotates to the left, the ball moves across to the right. Hence, in rotation the left foot needs to extend out and land on toes

THE BODY COACH

- As the ball rolls the body remains in contact with ball to control movement and speed
- The left leg reaches under and across to become shoulder width apart and resting on toes as the body rotates and stomach now rests on ball to complete a half-rotation (180°)
- Reverse movement pattern, rolling body and arms back to starting position by taking left leg back under right leg and out until resting on sole of foot and body once again on its back on the ball
- Repeat movement across to the right side – simultaneously take the right leg under the left leg and out into front support position whilst the body and arms rotate and once again you are lying on your stomach on the ball. Reverse movement pattern. Note: Rotating the arms to the right, makes the ball travel across to the left
- Repeat 180-degree half rotation to both sides, pausing at each end position to re-set the body position

Teaching Points

- Rotating arms to left the ball will travel to the right side and visa-versa
- Arms travel outside line of ball
- Use arms for balance in rotation
- Keep head in line with chest and arms in rotation
- Take movement slowly to maintain control and speed of motion
- Maintain contact of hip, back and stomach on ball in rotation for full control
- Ensure the feet rotate across to shoulder-width apart for essential support of the body
- The ball and body should rotate evenly and in a straight line
- Efficient timing of the body roll and feet placement is very important to ensure co-ordination, balance and stability
- Maintain deep breathing pattern throughout movement patterns

1. Start

2. Midpoint

3. 180° Rotation

4. Continue rotation

5. Complete 360° turn

Emphasis

- Muscular balance, co-ordination and timing in rotation

Description

- Lie on ball, supported under lower back
- Feet shoulder-width apart, arms extended out to the side, parallel to ground

THE BODY COACH

- Simultaneously turn chest and arms together to the left side whilst taking left leg under right leg in rotation
- As the body rotates to the left, the ball moves across to the right. Hence, in rotation the left foot needs to extend out and land on toes
- As the ball rolls the body remains in contact with ball to control movement and speed
- The left leg reaches under and across to become shoulder width apart and resting on toes as the body rotates and stomach now rests on ball to complete a half-rotation (180°)
- Continue rotation in same direction – from the stomach onto the side then back. The right leg moves under the body whilst rotating until shoulder-width apart and resting back on the foot print
- The body is once again on its back on the ball to complete one full 360° rotation
- Repeat rotation sequence in opposite direction

Teaching Points
- Rotating arms to left the ball will travel to the right side and visa-versa
- Arms travel outside line of ball
- Use arms for balance in rotation
- Keep head in line with chest and arms in rotation
- Take movement slowly to maintain control and speed of motion
- Maintain contact of hip, back and stomach on ball in rotation for full control
- Ensure the feet rotate across to shoulder-width apart for essential support of the body
- The ball and body should rotate evenly and in a straight line
- Efficient timing of the body roll and feet placement is very important to ensure co-ordination, balance and stability
- Maintain deep breathing pattern throughout movement patterns

Rotational test over 10m

Description

- Find a clear, flat, non-slip space with your coach, such as a football oval or indoor basketball court
- Mark out a 10metre distance. Use a line if available
- The objective is to travel at a controlled speed in a straight line for 10m – first to the left side over 10m.
- Rest and then repeat for 10m to the right side.

Objective

- Ones inability to control the speed or maintain a straight line may indicate muscle weakness or poor timing – areas to work on!
- Hence, practice 180-degree rotation to the left and right sides until competent, before attempting 360-degree rotation.
- A combination of abdominal, lower back and chest and arms exercises on the ball with help strengthen ones core and improve strength and co-ordination for this test

THE BODY COACH

Chapter 9

Stretching on the Ball

Stretching plays a vital role in exercise by assisting in maintaining good range of joint motion and muscle pliability. Stretching also helps increase muscle length and restore circulation. Stretching is beneficial after the muscles are warmed up. They can be performed throughout a training session and as a routine at the end to reduce muscle soreness developing.

The following exercises maybe used in association with general static stretches after warming up the muscles or warming down at the end of a training session:

- Hold each end position for up to 15 seconds.
- Keep stretches gentle, no pain should be present.
- Maintain deep breathing pattern throughout stretching. Do not hold your breath
- Repeat stretch three times in both directions, if appropriate

53

Prone Stretch

Lower back and pelvis

Description

- Lie across ball on stomach, bend knees and place hands on the ground for support
- Let the body relax to stretch the back, spine and pelvic regions

54

Supine Stretch

Spine

Description

- Lie on ball on back supported under lower back region
- Relax and extend arms overhead to stretch back and spine

THE BODY COACH

Chest and Shoulder

Chest and shoulder region

Description
- Kneel on ground next to ball
- Bend arm at 90-degree angle and place up onto ball in line with shoulders
- Gently lower body for stretch. Repeat opposite arm

Upper Back and Shoulders

Upper Back

Description
- Kneel on ground in front of ball
- Extend arms forward and gently sink through shoulders for stretch

57 Side Stretch

Reach to side

Description
- Sit on ball and brace abdominal muscles
- Place one hand on side of ball whilst extending the other arm overhead and across to the opposite side
- Repeat movement in opposite direction

58 Hamstrings

Hamstrings

Description
- Sit on ball and brace abdominal muscles
- Extend legs forward and straighten resting up on heels
- Keeping torso long gently lean forward for stretch

THE BODY COACH

Stretching Summary Chart

- Hold each end position for up to 15 seconds.
- Keep stretches gentle, no pain should be present.
- Maintain deep breathing pattern throughout stretching.
- Repeat stretch three times in both directions, if applicable.

53. Prone Stretch

54. Supine Stretch

55. Chest and Shoulder

56. Upper Back and Shoulders

57. Side Stretch

58. Hamstrings

Chapter 10

Developing A Fitness Ball Routine

A fitness ball routine supplements fitness training in a number of ways. It can be used as an exercise tool that primarily targets one area of the body such as the abdominal muscles or a number of muscle groups in a circuit format. It can also be used specifically for improving, balance and co-ordination or as a strength training routine using hand weights. On the other hand a whole body routine can be performed in the comfort of your own home or your local gym.

To get the ball rolling, it is important to start simple and master the basic exercise techniques and muscle control required by the body. All exercises should be performed slowly and in a controlled manner in order to effectively target muscles for toning and strengthening. The ability to hold good posture throughout the movement is vital as this ensures a good quality of movement is being maintained.

Every person will vary in his or her ability to perform the same exercise. What maybe seen as easy for one-person maybe be hard for another. As a result, the number of repetitions, sets and rest will need to be determined by a certified fitness professional or physiotherapist. Below are a series of sample fitness ball routines that focuses on 4 key areas of the body:

1. Abdominal region
2. Lower back and hip region – in rear support
3. Chest, arms and torso – in front support
4. Legs and hip

Note: *Additional Fitness Ball exercises are available in The Body Coach: Core-Strength Basics book. For more details visit: www.thebodycoach.com*

FITNESS BALL DRILLS

Determining Repetitions and Sets

The ideal number of repetitions (reps) varies between 8-12 and 12-15 reps, for strength and endurance respectively, and 3 sets per exercise. As muscle needs to be overloaded to stimulate growth, in body weight fitness ball training this is achieved through the hundreds of small adjustments the muscles need to make in order to control the exercise as well as a core-strength continuum. In lifting weights you simply add more weight to the bar or dumbbells, whereas it body weight training you can increase the intensity or overload by slowing down the time it takes to perform each repetition (i.e. from 2 seconds to 4 seconds), otherwise performing a more challenging exercise for the same muscle group – the goal of the core-strength continuum. As one exercise becomes easy, you move up the core-strength continuum to a harder exercise of the same muscle group. This may entail going from performing a push-up on the ground to having the feet resting on a fitness ball to increase the challenge. In other cases, it may require starting with harder exercises first and easy exercises later in the training so you fall within this 8–12 repetition range, as the exercises are much harder to perform from fatigue.

Overload in bodyweight fitness ball training can also come from rotating exercises and reducing the rest periods between sets. Time on task can also be used as a replacement of repetitions. As not one routine is one fits all, having various options available provides the variety required to achieve your goal. Ultimately it becomes a game of trial and error, as some participants will easily surpass the set amount of reps, where others fail. So, aim for the 8–12 repetition range. If you do it easy, change the exercise or simply slow the exercise down so you spend more time under tension. For example, if you can do 12 push-ups easy in 12 seconds, slow it down to perform up to 12 reps in 24 or 36 seconds (2 or 3 seconds each rep) maintaining good form and you will be challenged.

Ultimately, the variations supplied above will help establish the repetitions and sets to suit your needs for overloading a muscle group for optimal strength gains between muscle groups. Vary exercises regularly to maintain this challenge and always focus on improving the link between weaker and more dominant muscle groups throughout the body for better movement synergy.

Recovery or Rest Periods

Allowing 30–180 seconds recovery is recommended between most exercises, if working the same muscle group or the same exercise is being repeated.

Recovery is generally based on two key elements:

1. Purpose of your training – low (endurance: 15-60 seconds), medium (strength: 60-90 seconds) or high intensity (power: 90-180 seconds).

2. Ones current fitness or strength level.

The longer the recovery period the fresher you will be – choose accordingly. Stretching in-between exercises is recommended, whereas, when an athlete is involved in a circuit type format moving from one exercises straight to the next or one muscle group to another, adapting a low-intensity short rest period of only 15-30 seconds may apply.

Fill in the number of **sets, reps** and **rest** to suit your current training needs in the following fitness ball routines:

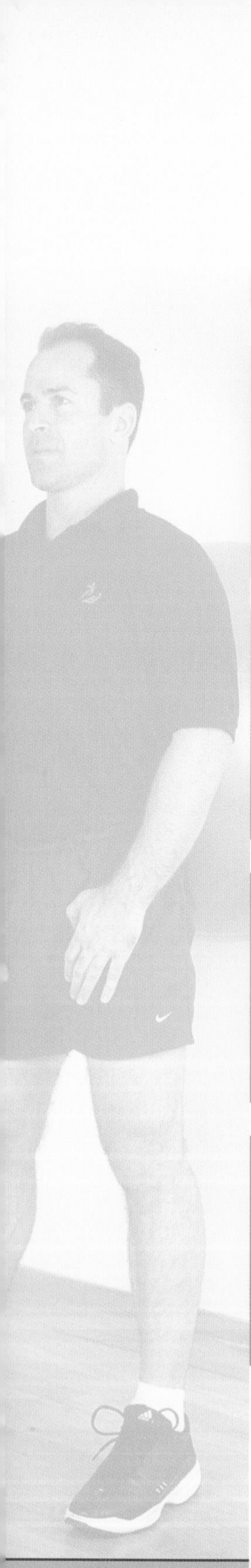

General Fitness Ball Routine

Exercise	Target Area

1. Single Knee Lift

Sets: _____
Reps: _____
Rest: _____

Balance

2. Supine Hip Extension

Sets: _____
Reps: _____
Rest: _____

Lower Back and Hip Extensors

3. Prone Walk-out

Sets: _____
Reps: _____
Rest: _____

Chest, Arms and Torso

4. Fitness Ball Squat

Sets: _____
Reps: _____
Rest: _____
Legs and Hip

Chest, Arms and Torso

Recommendation: All exercises must be performed under the guidance and supervision of a certified fitness professional or physiotherapist.

General Fitness Ball Routine

Exercise   **Target Area**

5. Abdominal Crunch – Short Lever

Sets: _____
Reps: _____
Rest: _____

Abdominal Muscles

6. Prone Isometric Holds

Sets: _____
Reps: _____ (time based exercise)
Rest: _____

Abdominal and Shoulders

7. Trunk Extension – Short Lever

Sets: _____
Reps: _____
Rest: _____

Lower Back

8. Hamstring Curls

Sets: _____
Reps: _____
Rest: _____
Hamstrings

Hamstrings

Recommendation: All exercises must be performed under the guidance and supervision of a certified fitness professional or physiotherapist.

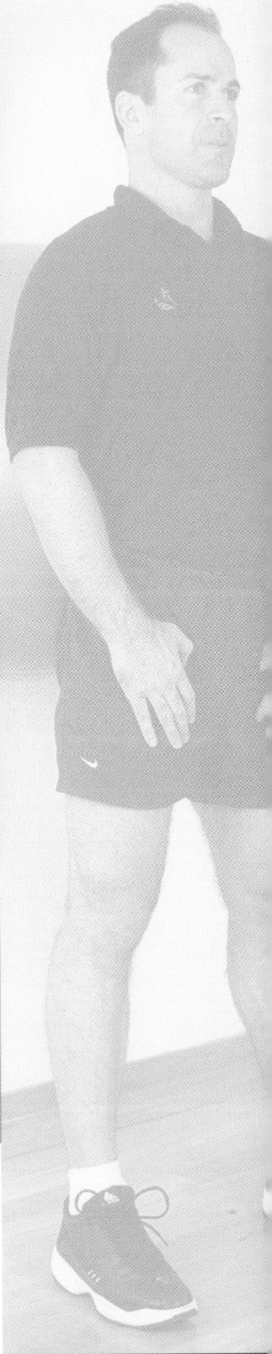

Beginner Level
Abdominal Core Routine

Exercise	Target Area

1. Knee Lift with Leg Extension

Sets: _____
Reps: _____
Rest: _____

Note: Repeat with opposite leg

Balance – Abdominal and Hip

2. Abdominal Roll-ups

Sets: _____
Reps: _____
Rest: _____

*Note: Add weight to hands
to extra resistance*

Abdominal Muscles

3. Abdominal Reach

Sets: _____
Reps: _____
Rest: _____

Abdominal Muscles

4. Trunk Extension –
Short Lever

Sets: _____
Reps: _____
Rest: _____

Lower Back

Recommendation: All exercises must be performed under the guidance
and supervision of a certified fitness professional or physiotherapist.

THE BODY COACH

Intermediate Level
Abdominal Core Routine

Exercise	Target Area

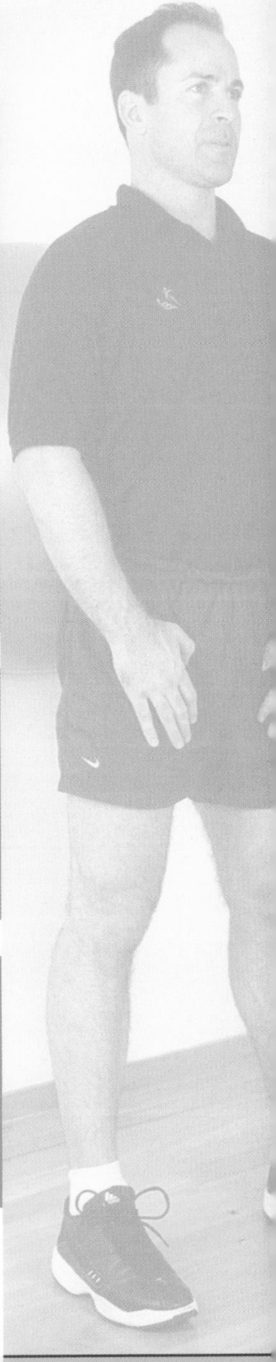

1. Abdominal Crunch –
Short Lever

Sets: _____
Reps: _____
Rest: _____

Abdominal Muscles

2. Oblique Twist

Sets: _____
Reps: _____
Rest: _____

*Note: Add weight to hands
for added resistance*

Abdominal Oblique Muscles

3. Prone Roll-out –
Short Lever

Sets: _____
Reps: _____
Rest: _____

Chest, Arms, Torso

4. Alternate Raises

Sets: _____
Reps: _____
Rest: _____

Shoulder and Obliques

Recommendation: All exercises must be performed under the guidance
and supervision of a certified fitness professional or physiotherapist.

Advanced Level
Abdominal Core Routine

Exercise	Target Area

1. Abdominal Crunch – Long Lever

Sets: _____
Reps: _____
Rest: _____

Abdominal Muscles

2. Oblique Cross-over

Sets: _____
Reps: _____
Rest: _____

Note: Repeat on opposite side

Abdominal Oblique Muscles

3. Prone Walk-out

Sets: _____
Reps: _____
Rest: _____

Chest, Abdominal, Hip

4. Side Support – Left and Right Side

Sets: _____
Reps: _____ (time based exercise)
Rest: _____

Note: Repeat with opposite arm

Shoulder and Obliques

Recommendation: All exercises must be performed under the guidance and supervision of a certified fitness professional or physiotherapist.

THE BODY COACH

Advanced Level
Abdominal Core Routine

Exercise	Target Area

5. Prone Jack-knife

Sets: _____
Reps: _____
Rest: _____

Chest, Abdominal, Hip

6. Prone Abdominal/Hip Raise

Sets: _____
Reps: _____
Rest: _____

Shoulder and Abdominal

7. Push-ups

Sets: _____
Reps: _____
Rest: _____

Chest and Abdominal

8. Prone Roll-out – Short Lever

Sets: _____
Reps: _____
Rest: _____

Chest, Arms and Torso

Recommendation: All exercises must be performed under the guidance and supervision of a certified fitness professional or physiotherapist.

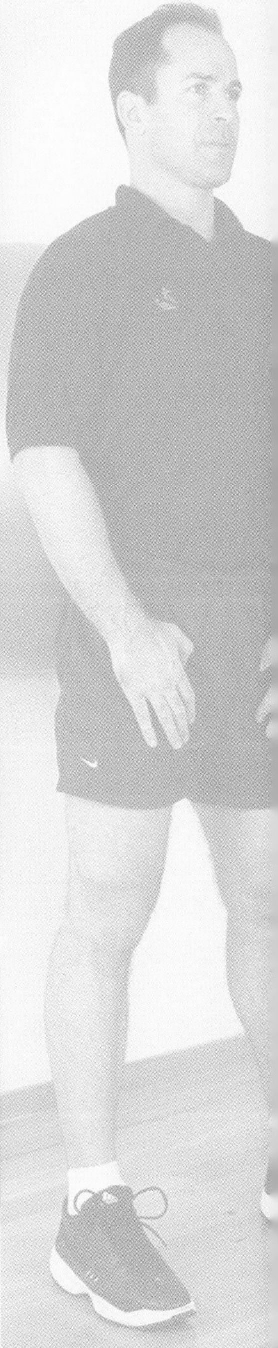

Fitness Ball Index

THE BODY COACH

Photo & Illustration Credits

Cover Photo: Paul Collins/Mark Donaldson
Cover Design: Jens Vogelsang
Other Photos: Paul Collins/
                Getty images

The Body Coach® – Products and Services

BOOK SERIES

The Body Coach® Book Series
- The Body Coach provides the latest cutting edge fitness training books written in a user-friendly format that is so advanced, that it's actually simple.

SEMINARS

The Body Coach® Keynotes and Seminars
- Corporate health and wellbeing keynote presentations
- Convention partner programs
- Seminars and Workshops
- Exclusive 5-star VIP Coaching – World-wide
- TV, Radio, interactive and Print Media Services

COURSES

The Body Coach® Programs and Courses
- Personal Training Certification Courses
- Continuing Education Courses (CEC)
- Licensed Group Fitness: Fastfeet®, Quickfeet®, Posturefit®, Swimstrength™, Kidstrength™
- Weight Loss Programs – Thigh Busters®, Belly Busters®, 3 Hour Rule®

PRODUCTS

Body Coach® Fitness Products and Brand Licensing
- Product Range – Speedhoop®, Spinal Unloading Block™, Muscle Mate®, Lumbatube™, Itibulator™, Rebound Medicine Ball™ & more...
- Product Education – Book and DVD Productions
- Product Brand Licensing opportunities

International Managing Agent

Saxton Speakers Bureau (Australia)

- Website: www.saxton.com.au
- Email: speakers@saxton.com.au
- Phone: (03) 9811 3500
  International: +61 3 9811 3500

www.thebodycoach.com

Study in Australia

- International Fitness College for overseas students to study sport, fitness and personal training qualifications in Sydney Australia
- 3 month to 2 year student visa courses

www.sportandfitness.com.au